AUDREY GRANT BRIDGE GUIDE

DECLARER PLAY SERIES 2

FIVE TIPS TO SIMPLIFY CARD COMBINATIONS

A Practical Approach to Improve the Odds

Audrey Grant

Five Tips to Simplify Card Combinations
A Practical Approach to Improve the Odds

Baron Barclay
3600 Chamberlain Lane, Suite 206
Louisville, KY 40241
U.S. and Canada: 1-800-274-2221
Worldwide: 502-426-0140
Fax: 502-426-2044
www.baronbarclay.com

Contact the author at:
betterbridge@betterbridge.com

ISBN 978-1-944201-21-0

Design and composition by David Lindop

Printed in the United States of America

Contents

Introduction

This Bridge Guide simplifies card combinations, making them accessible to players with a wide range of experience and skill. It's a practical book because the combinations are seen in the context of an entire deal.

PART I – AN INTRODUCTION TO THE FIVE TIPS

In each of the five segments, a tip is introduced. Deals are included in Part I to illustrate the tips.

PART II - A COLLECTION OF INSTRUCTIONAL DEALS

The basic and finer points of card combinations are introduced through sixteen carefully constructed deals. The first in the collection is straightforward yet complete with the basic ideas about handling card combinations. The deals become more challenging. Deals #15 and #16, the Famous Deals, show how world-class players handle card combinations.

THE BRIDGE QUIZ

On the odd-numbered pages, the Instructional Deals are shown in a Bridge Quiz format. The Suggested Bidding, Opening Lead, and the first steps in Planning the Play are given. The Bridge Quiz poses a challenge for the declarer to decide how to play the deal. Turn the page to see the Suggested Play and the Conclusion.

BOOKMARKS

Essential ideas are summarized on the four bookmarks.

The Declarer's Plan bookmark can help declarer make a habit of using the plan before playing to the first trick. This bookmark can be placed over the even-numbered pages, starting on page 20, opposite the Bridge Quiz on page 21.

The bookmark, Five Tips to Simplify Card Combinations, can be placed over the odd-numbered pages when reading the answer to a Bridge Quiz as a reminder of the specific tip being applied.

There are two reference bookmarks: one is the Probability of Suit Distributions in the Defenders' Hands and the other is Combinations Providing More Than a 50% Chance of Success.

OPENING LEAD GUIDELINES

Declarer reviews the auction and analyzes the opening lead when implementing Declarer's Plan. For your convenience, standard Opening Lead Guidelines are included on page 53.

THE GLOSSARY

Italicized words in the text are defined in the Glossary, with page references for where the terms first appear.

THE PUBLISHING

The Audrey Grant Bridge Guide series is published with the reader in mind. The two-color printing highlights the hearts and diamonds in red, making the book easier to read. The specific binding method allows the front and back covers to be put together without harming the book. This makes it possible for the book to lay flat on the table.

We hope you enjoy your adventure with card combinations. Thank you for being part of Better Bridge.

Audrey Grant and the Better Bridge Team

PART I

AN INTRODUCTION TO THE FIVE TIPS

Make a Plan

Card combinations are traditionally discussed by looking at a combined holding in a single suit, to consider how to get a specific number of tricks. The possibility for reaching the goal is expressed in a percentage. The auction isn't given, and it's assumed there are no problems with *entries* or the opponents.

Consider this card combination which comes up in many deals:

DUMMY (NORTH)
♥ A Q 7

DECLARER (SOUTH)
♥ 9 6 4

There is one *sure trick*, the ♥A. Declarer can try to get a second trick by leading a heart toward dummy and *finessing* the ♥Q. This has a 50% chance of success. If West holds the ♥K, the finesse will succeed, and declarer has two tricks. If East holds the ♥K, the finesse will lose and declarer is back to one trick.

The Encyclopedia of Bridge suggests the following: lead low away from the ace-queen, in case East has a singleton king. If East doesn't have the singleton king, nothing is lost. You can still play low toward the ♥A-Q combination. It is also a good idea in this layout:

DUMMY (NORTH)
♥ A Q 7

WEST
♥ J 10 8 3 2

EAST
♥ K 5

DECLARER (SOUTH)
♥ 9 6 4

If declarer starts with a low heart from dummy, it's possible East will play the ♥K, afraid of not getting a trick with it. Now declarer has two tricks with the ♥A-Q.

The most practical way to handle card combinations is to consider them in the context of the entire deal, not in isolation. With that in mind the first tip is to start with *Declarer's Plan*.

ASSESS THE SITUATION

When the opening lead is made, and dummy appears, declarer should make a plan before playing the first card from dummy. Declarer starts by counting the sure *winners* in a notrump contract and comparing the total to the number of tricks needed. In a suit contract, declarer typically starts by counting the possible *losers*.

BROWSE DECLARER'S CHECKLIST

If there are not enough tricks to make the contract, extra tricks can be developed in notrump or suit contracts through *promotion*, *length* and the finesse. In a suit contract, declarer has the additional options of *trumping* or *discarding* losers.

CONSIDER THE ORDER

Declarer decides the order to play the cards based on: the number of tricks required, entries, handling trumps, and the opponents.

Consider the first example:

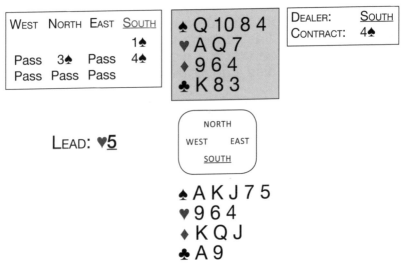

WEST	NORTH	EAST	SOUTH
			1♠
Pass	3♠	Pass	4♠
Pass	Pass	Pass	

♠ Q 10 8 4
♥ A Q 7
♦ 9 6 4
♣ K 8 3

DEALER: SOUTH
CONTRACT: 4♠

LEAD: ♥5

NORTH
WEST   EAST
SOUTH

♠ A K J 7 5
♥ 9 6 4
♦ K Q J
♣ A 9

Before making the decision of what heart to play at trick one, declarer starts with a plan and considers the potential losers: no spades, two hearts, one diamond, and no clubs. Declarer has three losers and, in 4♠, can afford to lose three tricks. Declarer doesn't need to eliminate a loser and plays the ♥A at trick one to secure the contract.

The value of making a plan before playing to the first trick can be seen when this is the complete deal:

DEALER:	SOUTH
CONTRACT:	4♠

♠ Q 10 8 4
♥ A Q 7
♦ 9 6 4
♣ K 8 3

♠ 9 3 2
♥ 5
♦ 10 8 3 2
♣ Q 7 6 4 2

NORTH
WEST   EAST
SOUTH

♠ 6
♥ K J 10 8 3 2
♦ A 7 5
♣ J 10 5

♠ A K J 7 5
♥ 9 6 4
♦ K Q J
♣ A 9

Winning the ♥A from dummy at trick one doesn't cost anything even if West did start with the ♥K. After drawing trumps, declarer can still lead a heart toward dummy's ♥Q to try to make an overtrick.

If, however, declarer plays the ♥Q at trick one, East wins the ♥K and returns a high heart, the ♥J. This is a *suit preference signal*, asking West to play a diamond rather than a club, after trumping the heart trick.

West ruffs the ♥J, and leads a diamond to East's ♦A. East leads another heart for West to ruff. The 4♠ contract is down one.

Let's look at another deal, this time in 6♠.

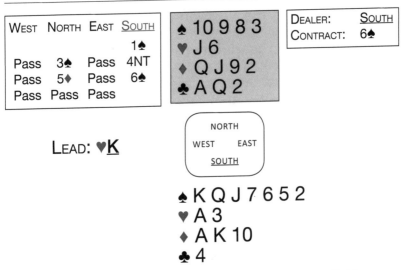

LEAD: ♥K

Declarer makes a plan and counts the potential losers: one spade, one heart, no diamonds, and no clubs. To make the slam, declarer needs to eliminate one loser. The heart loser could be discarded on dummy's extra diamond winner, but there's a problem. Declarer would first need to draw trumps to prevent the defenders from ruffing a diamond. As soon as declarer leads a trump, however, the opponents can win the ♠A and take the established heart winner.

The only alternative is for declarer to win the ♥A and immediately lead the singleton club and finesse dummy's ♣Q. The finesse wins and declarer discards the heart loser on the ♣A. This is a 50% finesse.

These two deals illustrate that, if you have the tricks you need, taking a finesse for an extra trick could give the defenders a chance to defeat the contract. If you need a finesse to make the contract, take it, even if it creates an extra loser if it doesn't work. The goal is to make the contract.

The first tip to simplify card combinations is:

Tip #1:   Use Declarer's Plan to decide how to play card combinations.

Combine Chances

If there are not enough tricks to make the contract, declarer browses Declarer's Checklist and looks at each suit in turn for opportunities to get the extra tricks needed. For quick reference here is the checklist.

Declarer's Checklist	
Promotion	
Length	
Finesse	
Trumping Losers	
Discarding Losers	

When there is only one possibility, declarer has to go with that. Whenever possible, declarer combines the chances to increase the odds of making the contract.

Consider these two card combinations:

1) Dummy (North)
♥ A Q 7

West
♥ K 5 2

East
♥ J 10 8 3

Declarer (South)
♥ 9 6 4

2) Dummy (North)
♥ Q 7 4

West
♥ K 5 2

East
♥ J 10 8 3

Declarer (South)
♥ A 9 6

There are exactly the same cards in each combination. There is one trick with the ♥A and a 50% possibility of developing an extra trick with the ♥Q. The difference is that, in the first example, declarer doesn't have to give up a trick if the finesse works because the ♥A-Q in dummy can capture the ♥K.

In the second example, the finesse also works, even though West has the option of taking the ♥K before the ♥Q in dummy becomes a winner.

Consider the following deal. South is in 6NT and West leads the ♠10.

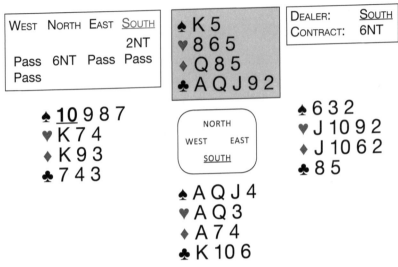

West	North	East	South
			2NT
Pass	6NT	Pass	Pass
Pass			

Dealer: South
Contract: 6NT

♠ K 5
♥ 8 6 5
♦ Q 8 5
♣ A Q J 9 2

♠ 10 9 8 7
♥ K 7 4
♦ K 9 3
♣ 7 4 3

NORTH
WEST   EAST
SOUTH

♠ 6 3 2
♥ J 10 9 2
♦ J 10 6 2
♣ 8 5

♠ A Q J 4
♥ A Q 3
♦ A 7 4
♣ K 10 6

Assess the Situation. There are eleven winners: four spades, one heart, one diamond, and five clubs. One more trick is needed.

Browse Declarer's Checklist. Declarer isn't getting more tricks from spades or clubs. In hearts, there is a 50% chance of a finesse if East holds the ♥K. In diamonds, there is also a 50% chance of a finesse if West holds the ♦K. Declarer wants to try both finesses to provide a 75% chance of success.

It's usually better to "take losses early." So, declarer starts by leading a low diamond toward the ♦Q in dummy. The diamond finesse works and the ♦Q is the twelfth trick, even if West wins the first diamond trick with the ♦K. If the finesse lost, declarer could still try the heart finesse.

Suppose declarer starts with the heart finesse and it loses. It's too late for declarer to try the diamond finesse because West would take the ♦K as the setting trick.

The second tip to simplify card combinations is:

Tip #2:   Browse Declarer's Checklist if you need more tricks. Combine chances, taking the losses early if necessary.

Know the Best Odds

When declarer has more than one possibility to create an extra winner or eliminate a loser and can't combine the chances, declarer chooses the card combination that offers the best odds for success. There are too many combinations to memorize the probability in each case, but some general guidelines are worth remembering.

DEVELOPING WINNERS THROUGH THE FINESSE

A finesse requiring one of the defenders' cards to be favorably located typically has a 50% chance of success.

In the following example, declarer hopes West holds the ♠A and leads toward the ♠K in dummy.

DUMMY (NORTH)
♠ K 7 3

DECLARER (SOUTH)
♠ 6 4 2

In the next example, declarer is missing two cards, the ♥K and ♥Q, yet there is a 75% chance of developing an extra trick because declarer can take a repeated finesse.

DUMMY (NORTH)
♥ A J 10

DECLARER (SOUTH)
♥ 6 4 2

First, declarer leads low toward dummy, playing the ♥J or ♥10. If this loses to the ♥K or ♥Q, declarer later repeats the finesse, leading low toward dummy again.

Playing this way, declarer gets an extra trick if the cards are favorably placed and West holds the ♥K, or the ♥Q, or both the ♥K and ♥Q. Only if East holds both the ♥K and ♥Q will declarer fail to get an extra trick. Declarer will succeed in three out of four cases, 75% of the time.

ESTABLISHING TRICKS THROUGH LENGTH

Declarer looks to develop extra tricks through length, giving up one or more tricks to the opponents if necessary.

A useful guideline is:

- An odd number of missing cards tend to divide as evenly as possible.
- An even number of missing cards tend to divide slightly unevenly.

Consider the following example:

DUMMY (NORTH)
♥ A 6 5

DECLARER (SOUTH)
♥ K 7 4 3 2

Declarer has eight hearts in the combined hands, leaving the opponents with five. The odds favor the missing five cards being divided 3-2, as evenly as possible. The actual odds are 67.8%, that's better than a 50% finesse. Declarer can play the ♥A and ♥K and give up a trick to the opponents. Declarer's remaining two hearts will then be winners. Declarer could also give up a trick first, taking the losses early, and then play the ♥A and ♥K.

Consider the next example:

DUMMY (NORTH)
♣ 5 4 3 2

DECLARER (SOUTH)
♣ A K Q

The odds favor the missing six cards being divided 4-2, slightly unevenly. To get an extra trick, the hearts would have to be divided exactly 3-3, a 35.5% chance. That's less than the odds of a 50% finesse. The various divisions of missing cards can be found on the bookmark: Probability of Suit Distributions in the Defenders' Hands.

Let's look at an example showing the best odds in a complete deal.

West leads the ♠Q against South's 3NT contract. What is declarer's plan?

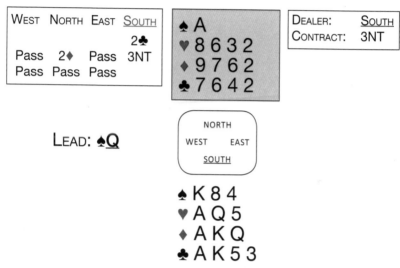

West	North	East	South
			2♣
Pass	2♦	Pass	3NT
Pass	Pass	Pass	

♠ A
♥ 8 6 3 2
♦ 9 7 6 2
♣ 7 6 4 2

Dealer: South
Contract: 3NT

Lead: ♠Q

NORTH
WEST   EAST
SOUTH

♠ K 8 4
♥ A Q 5
♦ A K Q
♣ A K 5 3

Assess the Situation. There are eight immediate winners: two spades, one heart, three diamonds, and two clubs. One more trick is needed.

Browse Declarer's Checklist. There is a 50% possibility of a heart finesse working if East holds the ♥K. There are better odds in the club suit. Declarer can get an extra trick through length if the defenders' clubs are divided 3-2, by giving up a club trick. The odds of that are 67.8%.

West's ♠Q lead removes the ♠A, the only entry to dummy. Declarer has to decide right away between taking the heart finesse, a 50% chance, or developing a trick through length in the club suit, a 67.8% chance, giving up a club trick. The odds favor playing clubs.

After winning the ♠A, declarer should play the ♣A, ♣K, and if both defenders have followed suit twice, a third round of clubs. Although this trick is lost to the opponents, the fourth club is set up as a winner.

Here's the complete deal:

DEALER:	SOUTH
CONTRACT:	3NT

North
- ♠ A
- ♥ 8 6 3 2
- ♦ 9 7 6 2
- ♣ 7 6 4 2

West
- ♠ Q J 10 7 5
- ♥ K 7 4
- ♦ 8 5
- ♣ Q 10 8

East
- ♠ 9 6 3 2
- ♥ J 10 9
- ♦ J 10 4 3
- ♣ J 9

South
- ♠ K 8 4
- ♥ A Q 5
- ♦ A K Q
- ♣ A K 5 3

If declarer wins the ♠A and starts with the heart finesse, it loses to West's ♥K. West continues spades, driving out the ♠K and establishing the spade suit. Now it is too late to give up a club because the defenders will get three spades, a heart, and a club. Instead, declarer has to go with the odds and give up a club trick right away, hoping the defenders' clubs are divided 3-2. Then the fourth club is established as a winner before the defenders promote the spade winners.

PROMOTING TRICKS

Promotion is 100% to get extra tricks. There are, however, considerations. To get to promoted winners, entries are necessary. Since promotion requires giving up a trick or two, declarer has to make sure the opponents are safe and can't defeat the contract if they get the lead.

The third tip to simplify card combinations is:

Tip #3:   Look for card combinations that provide more than a 50% chance of getting extra tricks.

Know When to Lead a High Card

In some card combinations, declarer can lead an *honor*, and afford to have it covered, when trying to trap the opponents' high cards.

Consider this heart layout:

DUMMY (NORTH)
♥ A 4 3

WEST
♥ K 6 2

EAST
♥ 9 8 7 5

DECLARER (SOUTH)
♥ Q J 10

Declarer leads a high heart, hoping to trap the ♥K in West's hand. If West doesn't play the ♥K, South's heart wins the trick. If West does cover with the ♥K, declarer's ♥A, and the remaining hearts in South's hand, are winners. Declarer gets three tricks 50% of the time. If East has the ♥K, however, the finesse loses and declarer gets only two tricks.

Consider this layout:

DUMMY (NORTH)
♥ A 4 3

WEST
♥ J 10 9 8

EAST
♥ K 7 5

DECLARER (SOUTH)
♥ Q 6 2

To get two heart tricks from this combination, East, not West, must hold the ♥K. Declarer can get a second trick by leading a low heart from dummy toward the ♥Q. The ♥K can take a trick, but it can't capture the ♥Q.

If instead South leads the ♥Q, it would be captured by East's ♥K, and declarer would get only one trick. South, with the ♥Q-6-2, missing the ♥J-10, doesn't have the strength to lead a high card.

In the next example, there are two tricks available for declarer and it doesn't matter whether declarer leads a high card or leads toward it.

DUMMY (NORTH)
♥ A 4 3

WEST   EAST
♥ K 7 5   ♥ 10 9 8 6

DECLARER (SOUTH)
♥ Q J 2

Suppose declarer starts by leading the ♥Q, and West covers with the ♥K. Dummy's ♥A can win the first trick, and the ♥J in declarer's hand can win the second trick. The third trick will be won with the ♥10 in East's hand. If declarer leads low from the dummy toward the ♥Q-J, declarer plays a high heart, and West takes the trick with the ♥K. Declarer still gets two tricks.

However, if declarer needs two heart tricks but can't afford to let the opponents gain the lead, declarer has to lead the ♥Q, or ♥J, hoping West holds the ♥K.

Consider this diamond layout:

DUMMY (NORTH)
♦ Q J 6 2

WEST   EAST
♦ 10 9 5 4   ♦ K 8

DECLARER (SOUTH)
♦ A 7 3

Although it is tempting to lead the ♦Q to hopefully trap the ♦K in East's hand, declarer can't afford to have the ♦Q covered. If East does have the ♦K, declarer will only get two tricks since the opponents have both the ♦10 and ♦9. Declarer will now need the defenders' six diamonds to be divided 3-3 to get a third trick – and that's less than a 50% chance.

Let's look at a complete deal where North and South have the same diamonds as the previous example, but the ♦K is held by West rather than East.

West	North	East	South
			1NT
Pass	3NT	Pass	Pass
Pass			

♠ 6 4 3
♥ A 8
♦ Q J 6 2
♣ Q J 8 5

Dealer: South
Contract: 3NT

♠ K 5
♥ Q J 10 7 5
♦ K 10 9 5
♣ 6 4

NORTH
WEST   EAST
SOUTH

♠ A Q 7 2
♥ 9 4 3
♦ 8 4
♣ 9 7 3 2

♠ J 10 9 8
♥ K 6 2
♦ A 7 3
♣ A K 10

Assess the Situation. There are seven immediate winners: two hearts, one diamond, and four clubs. Two more tricks are needed.

Browse Declarer's Checklist. Declarer isn't getting more tricks from hearts or clubs and won't be able to establish a spade trick before the defenders can establish and take their heart winners. The extra tricks must come from diamonds.

If declarer leads the ♦Q from dummy, the finesse will lose to West's ♦K. The ♦J will be promoted into a winner, but West's ♦10 will win the fourth round of the suit.

If declarer plays the ♦A first, then leads a low diamond toward dummy, the ♦J will win if West plays low. Declarer can come back and lead the remaining diamond toward dummy. West can't prevent declarer from also getting a trick with the ♦Q.

This way gives declarer three diamond tricks if West holds the ♦K, or East holds a singleton ♦K, and any time East holds the ♦K but the defenders' diamonds are divided 3-3. Declarer has nearly a 70% chance of making the contract.

In summary, leading low toward an honor is usually a good idea, unless there is a group of honors, as in the first example with the ♥Q-J-10.

The fourth tip to simplify card combinations is:

Tip #4:   Avoid leading a high card if you can't afford to have it covered with a higher-raking card.

Watch Out for the Opponents

The defenders are trying to take enough tricks to defeat the contract. Declarer has to be aware of how the defenders are planning to take tricks and try to reduce their trick-taking potential. Sometimes, both defenders are *dangerous opponents* and all declarer can do is avoid the suit. Consider this layout of the diamond suit in a 3NT contract.

DUMMY (NORTH)
♦ A 6

WEST
♦ K Q J 7 2

EAST
♦ 10 9 5 4

DECLARER (SOUTH)
♦ 8 3

In this situation, both opponents are dangerous. After the ♦A is driven out, if either defender gets the lead and plays a diamond, the contract can be defeated.

Sometimes declarer has a *safe opponent* who can't make a lead that could defeat the contract.

Now, consider this diamond suit in a 4♠ contract:

DUMMY (NORTH)
♦ 8 2

WEST
♦ A Q J 4

EAST
♦ 10 9 6 5 3

DECLARER (SOUTH)
♦ K 7

In this layout, the ♦K is safe if West has the lead. If West plays the ♦A, the ♦K is a winner on the next trick. If West leads a low diamond, the ♦K wins the trick right away.

East is the dangerous opponent because if East gets the lead and plays a diamond, the defenders can capture the ♦K and take two diamond tricks.

THE HOLD-UP PLAY

The declarer can create a safe opponent by using a technique referred to as the *hold-up play*.

Consider this example:

DUMMY (NORTH)
♥ A 8 4

WEST
♥ K J 7 5 3

EAST
♥ Q 10 2

DECLARER (SOUTH)
♥ 9 6

Suppose West leads the ♥5 against declarer's 3NT contract. If declarer plays the ♥A from dummy on the first trick and then has to give up the lead, both defenders are dangerous because either East or West could lead a heart. If, on the other hand, declarer uses the hold-up play and takes the third heart trick with the ♥A, declarer has created East as a safe opponent because East has no hearts left.

ESTABLISHING A SAFE OPPONENT

Sometimes declarer is in a position to establish which opponent is dangerous.

WEST	NORTH	EAST	SOUTH
			1NT
Pass	3NT	Pass	Pass
Pass			

DEALER:	SOUTH
CONTRACT:	3NT

♠ Q 6
♥ K 10 8
♦ J 10 8
♣ A Q J 9 5

♠ A J 9 5 2
♥ 7 6
♦ K 5 3
♣ 8 3 2

NORTH
WEST   EAST
SOUTH

♠ 10 8 3
♥ 9 5 3 2
♦ 9 4 2
♣ K 7 4

♠ K 7 4
♥ A Q J 4
♦ A Q 7 6
♣ 10 6

Assess the Situation: After the spade lead, declarer is going to get a spade trick and has four hearts, a diamond, and a club. Two more tricks are needed.

Browse Declarer's Checklist: Declarer can try the diamond finesse. If it works, declarer has three extra winners. If it loses, two winners have been established. Alternatively, declarer can try the club finesse. If it wins, declarer may have four extra winners. If it loses, declarer will have three extra winners.

If declarer plays a low spade from dummy at trick one and wins the ♠K, then both defenders become dangerous. If either defender gains the lead, the defense can take the established spade winners.

Instead, declarer makes the key play of the ♠Q from dummy at trick one to establish which opponent is dangerous. When the ♠Q wins, East becomes the dangerous opponent and West is the safe opponent. Declarer can safely try the diamond finesse. Even though the finesse loses, declarer has the two extra tricks needed and West can't continue spades without giving declarer a trick with the ♠K. If West shifts to a club, declarer should win the ♣A to avoid letting the dangerous opponent gain the lead.

If East had won the first trick when the ♠Q is played from dummy, declarer could then hold up winning the ♠K until the third round. Now declarer would take the club finesse. If the finesse loses, the contract will be safe. If East still has a spade to lead, West will have started with only a four-card spade suit and the defense can't get more than three spade tricks.

QUICK AND SLOW LOSERS

Declarer needs to be aware of the difference between *quick* and *slow losers*. A quick loser is a trick the opponents are ready to take upon gaining the lead. A slow loser is a trick that may eventually have to be lost but that the opponents can't immediately take upon gaining the lead.

If declarer has too many quick losers and cannot afford to give the opponents the lead, declarer cannot develop extra tricks through promotion, where giving up a trick is essential.

The fifth tip to simplify card combinations is:

Tip #5: Use the hold-up play to create a safe opponent. Recognize the difference between quick and slow losers.

PART II

A COLLECTION OF
INSTRUCTIONAL DEALS

Bridge Quiz Instructions

The Bridge Quiz for each deal is on the odd-numbered page. To complete a Bridge Quiz, read:

- Suggested Bidding
- Opening Lead
- Planning the Play

Then consider the question posed in the Bridge Quiz. For the answer, turn the page to read:

- Suggested Play
- Conclusion

For reference, put the Declarer's Plan bookmark over the even-numbered page that faces the quiz on the odd-numbered page.

After deciding how to play each deal, turn the page over for the answer to the Bridge Quiz. Now put the Five Tips to Simplify Card Combinations bookmark, over the odd-numbered page that faces the answer as a reminder of the tip being applied.

In this Collection of Instructional Deals, declarer is always South, West makes the opening lead, and North is the dummy.

In deals #4, #10, #15, and #16, North is the dealer. In all other cases, South is the dealer.

DEAL #1

WEST	NORTH	EAST	SOUTH
			1NT
Pass	3NT	Pass	Pass
Pass			

♠ 8 5
♥ A Q 10
♦ K 10 7 3
♣ A 9 6 4

DEALER:	SOUTH
VUL:	NONE
CONTRACT:	3NT
DECLARER:	SOUTH

LEAD: ♥<u>6</u>

♠ K 4
♥ 8 5 3
♦ A Q J 8
♣ K Q J 5

SUGGESTED BIDDING

South opens 1NT with 16 high-card points and a balanced hand. North has 13 high-card points, enough to take the partnership to game. North raises to 3NT with no interest in a major suit.

OPENING LEAD

West leads the ♥6 against 3NT.

PLANNING THE PLAY

Declarer has to make a decision at trick one whether to play the ♥A, ♥Q or ♥10 to the first trick.

BRIDGE QUIZ:

What card from the dummy should declarer play to the first trick?

DEAL:	1
DEALER:	SOUTH
VUL:	NONE
CONTRACT:	3NT
DECLARER:	SOUTH

♠ 8 5
♥ A Q 10
♦ K 10 7 3
♣ A 9 6 4

3NT

NORTH

WEST   EAST

SOUTH

♠ A 9 6
♥ J 9 7 6 4 2
♦ 6 4
♣ 10 7

Pass	Pass

♠ Q J 10 7 3 2
♥ K
♦ 9 5 2
♣ 8 3 2

Pass

♠ K 4
♥ 8 5 3
♦ A Q J 8
♣ K Q J 5

1NT	Pass

SUGGESTED PLAY

Before making a decision to play the ♥A, ♥Q, or ♥10 to the first trick, use Declarer's Plan to Assess the Situation. Declarer has one sure heart trick, four diamonds, and four club tricks, a total of nine winners. No more tricks are needed. Declarer simply wins the ♥A and is rewarded when the ♥K falls under the ♥A.

Declarer doesn't give up getting an extra heart trick by playing the ♥A at trick one. After taking the first nine tricks, ending in the South hand, declarer can still lead a heart toward dummy's ♥Q-10. If West had held the ♥K, declarer would still get a trick with dummy's ♥Q by finessing after securing the contract. In the actual layout, declarer can now finesse the ♥10 and take eleven tricks.

CONCLUSION

If declarer tries the heart finesse at trick one, the defenders can defeat the contract. East wins the ♥K on the first trick and switches to the ♠Q, trapping declarer's ♠K. The defenders take the first seven tricks.

DEAL #2

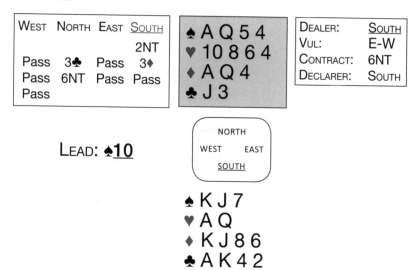

WEST	NORTH	EAST	SOUTH
			2NT
Pass	3♣	Pass	3♦
Pass	6NT	Pass	Pass
Pass			

♠ A Q 5 4
♥ 10 8 6 4
♦ A Q 4
♣ J 3

DEALER:	SOUTH
VUL:	E-W
CONTRACT:	6NT
DECLARER:	SOUTH

LEAD: ♠10

NORTH
WEST   EAST
SOUTH

♠ K J 7
♥ A Q
♦ K J 8 6
♣ A K 4 2

SUGGESTED BIDDING

South opens 2NT, with 21 high-card points and a balanced hand. North has 13 high-card points, enough to take the partnership to slam. First, North uses the *Stayman convention* to see if partner has a four-card major suit. When South replies 3♦, showing no major suit, North bids 6NT.

OPENING LEAD

West leads the ♠10 against 6NT.

PLANNING THE PLAY

Declarer has four sure spade tricks, one heart, four diamonds, and two clubs. That's eleven total winners. One more trick is needed.

BRIDGE QUIZ:

In what order should declarer play hearts and clubs to have a 75% chance of making the contract?

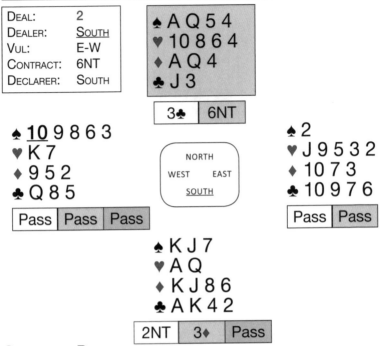

DEAL:	2
DEALER:	SOUTH
VUL:	E-W
CONTRACT:	6NT
DECLARER:	SOUTH

♠ A Q 5 4
♥ 10 8 6 4
♦ A Q 4
♣ J 3

| 3♣ | 6NT |

♠ 10 9 8 6 3
♥ K 7
♦ 9 5 2
♣ Q 8 5

NORTH
WEST   EAST
SOUTH

♠ 2
♥ J 9 5 3 2
♦ 10 7 3
♣ 10 9 7 6

| Pass | Pass | Pass |

| Pass | Pass |

♠ K J 7
♥ A Q
♦ K J 8 6
♣ A K 4 2

| 2NT | 3♦ | Pass |

SUGGESTED PLAY

To have a 75% chance of making 6NT, declarer has to try both the heart and club finesses. The order is important; declarer has to start with the club finesse.

Declarer leads a low club toward dummy's ♣J. If West holds the ♣Q, dummy's ♣J becomes a winner. Declarer can afford to lose one trick. On the actual deal, that works, and declarer has a twelfth trick with the ♣J, even if West takes the ♣Q first.

If East held the ♣Q, the finesse wouldn't work because East's ♣Q would take the ♣J. Declarer could then fall back on the heart finesse. If declarer starts with the heart finesse and it fails – as on the actual deal – it's too late to lead toward the ♣J. West would win the ♣Q as the second trick for the defense, defeating 6NT.

CONCLUSION

If declarer tries the heart finesse first, the contract can be defeated. Trying the club finesse first, taking the losses early, improves the odds from 50% to 75%.

DEAL #3

WEST	NORTH	EAST	SOUTH
			2NT
Pass	3NT	Pass	Pass
Pass			

♠ 9 5 3
♥ A 6
♦ 8 7 6 3
♣ A 5 3 2

DEALER:	SOUTH
VUL:	NONE
CONTRACT:	3NT
DECLARER:	SOUTH

LEAD: ♥J

♠ A J 10
♥ K 4
♦ A Q 4 2
♣ K Q J 6

SUGGESTED BIDDING

South opens 2NT with a balanced hand and 20 high-card points. North, with 8 high-card points, raises to 3NT.

OPENING LEAD

West leads the ♥J against 3NT.

PLANNING THE PLAY

Declarer starts with eight tricks: one spade, two hearts, one diamond, and four club winners. Declarer needs one more trick to make the contract.

BRIDGE QUIZ:

Which suit gives declarer the best chance to get one extra trick and make the contract?

DEAL:	3
DEALER:	SOUTH
VUL:	NONE
CONTRACT:	3NT
DECLARER:	SOUTH

♠ 9 5 3
♥ A 6
♦ 8 7 6 3
♣ A 5 3 2

3NT

♠ Q 4 2
♥ J 10 9 2
♦ K J 5
♣ 9 7 4

Pass | Pass

NORTH

WEST   EAST

SOUTH

♠ K 8 7 6
♥ Q 8 7 5 3
♦ 10 9
♣ 10 8

Pass

♠ A J 10
♥ K 4
♦ A Q 4 2
♣ K Q J 6

2NT | Pass

SUGGESTED PLAY

One possibility to get the extra trick is the diamond finesse, hoping East holds the ♦K. That's a 50% chance.

The other possibility is the repeated spade finesse, a 75% chance. Declarer starts by leading a low spade to the ♠A-J-10 combination, planning to play the ♠J or ♠10 on the first trick. Declarer expects to lose the first spade finesse. When declarer gets the lead again, declarer repeats the spade finesse, expecting that it will work. Spades provide an extra trick if East holds the ♠K, or the ♠Q, or both the ♠K and ♠Q. It only loses if West holds both the ♠K and ♠Q. This gives declarer a 75% chance of making an extra trick. Declarer should go with the odds and try the repeated spade finesse.

CONCLUSION

If declarer tries the diamond finesse, West can win the ♦K and lead another heart to establish the heart suit. It's then too late for declarer to give up the lead to try the repeated spade finesse.

DEAL #4

WEST	NORTH	EAST	SOUTH
	1♣	Pass	1♥
Pass	2♥	Pass	4♥
Pass	Pass	Pass	

♠ 6 2
♥ K J 7 2
♦ K 5 3
♣ A Q 6 2

DEALER:	NORTH
VUL:	E-W
CONTRACT:	4♥
DECLARER:	SOUTH

LEAD: ♦Q

NORTH
WEST   EAST
SOUTH

♠ A K
♥ A Q 10 4 3
♦ 9 6 2
♣ J 5 3

SUGGESTED BIDDING

North, with 13 high-card points and a balanced hand, is too weak to open 1NT and opens 1♣, the longer minor. South responds 1♥. North, with four-card heart support, revalues the hand, adding 1 dummy point for the doubleton spade. That's still a minimum hand, and North raises to 2♥. South, with 14 high-card points plus 1 length point for the five-card heart suit, has enough to go right to game after finding the heart fit.

OPENING LEAD

West leads the ♦Q against 4♥.

PLANNING THE PLAY

The defenders take the first three diamond tricks. Declarer can afford no more losers.

BRIDGE QUIZ:

How can declarer avoid losing a club trick?

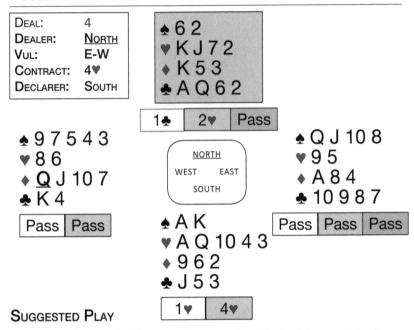

DEAL:	4
DEALER:	NORTH
VUL:	E-W
CONTRACT:	4♥
DECLARER:	SOUTH

♠ 6 2
♥ K J 7 2
♦ K 5 3
♣ A Q 6 2

| 1♣ | 2♥ | Pass |

♠ 9 7 5 4 3
♥ 8 6
♦ Q J 10 7
♣ K 4

NORTH
WEST   EAST
SOUTH

♠ Q J 10 8
♥ 9 5
♦ A 8 4
♣ 10 9 8 7

| Pass | Pass |

♠ A K
♥ A Q 10 4 3
♦ 9 6 2
♣ J 5 3

| Pass | Pass | Pass |

| 1♥ | 4♥ |

SUGGESTED PLAY

West's ♦Q lead indicates East probably holds the ♦A since most players avoid leading away from an ace against a suit contract. South's best chance to avoid a diamond loser is to play low from dummy, on both the first and second diamond tricks, hoping East started with a singleton or doubleton ♦A.

On this deal, the opponents take the first three diamond tricks. Declarer must now avoid losing a club trick. Declarer's only chance is that West started with either a singleton or doubleton ♣K.

Declarer draws trumps ending in declarer's hand and leads a low club to dummy's ♣Q. When this wins, declarer plays the ♣A. West's ♣K falls on the second round of clubs and declarer's ♣J is a winner. Declarer loses no club tricks.

CONCLUSION

If South plays the ♣J on the first club trick, West should play the ♣K, covering an honor with an honor. East will then get a trick with the ♣10 on the third round of clubs. Instead, declarer has to play a low club on the first trick, toward the ♣A-Q in dummy.

DEAL #5

WEST	NORTH	EAST	SOUTH
			1NT
Pass	3NT	Pass	Pass
Pass			

♠ Q 5
♥ A 8 4
♦ J 10 9
♣ A Q 9 5 4

DEALER:	SOUTH
VUL:	NONE
CONTRACT:	3NT
DECLARER:	SOUTH

LEAD: ♥**5**

♠ A K J
♥ 9 6
♦ A Q 8 6 3
♣ J 10 8

SUGGESTED BIDDING

South opens 1NT with 15 high-card points plus 1 length point for the five-card diamond suit. North has 13 high-card points plus 1 length point for the five-card club suit, enough for game. With no interest in a major-suit fit, North raises to 3NT.

OPENING LEAD

West leads the ♥5 against 3NT.

PLANNING THE PLAY

Declarer has three spades, a heart, a diamond, and a club. Three more tricks are needed to make the contract.

BRIDGE QUIZ:

Should declarer choose clubs or diamonds to develop the three tricks needed to make 3NT?

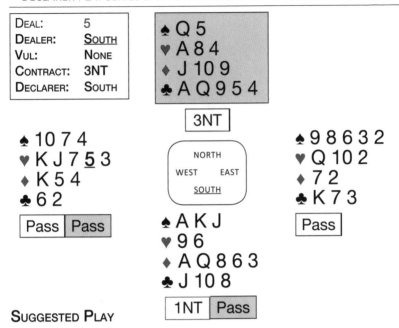

DEAL:	5
DEALER:	SOUTH
VUL:	NONE
CONTRACT:	3NT
DECLARER:	SOUTH

♠ Q 5
♥ A 8 4
♦ J 10 9
♣ A Q 9 5 4

3NT

NORTH
WEST   EAST
SOUTH

♠ 10 7 4
♥ K J 7 5 3
♦ K 5 4
♣ 6 2

Pass Pass

♠ 9 8 6 3 2
♥ Q 10 2
♦ 7 2
♣ K 7 3

Pass

♠ A K J
♥ 9 6
♦ A Q 8 6 3
♣ J 10 8

1NT Pass

SUGGESTED PLAY

If either the diamond or the club finesse works, declarer will have four additional tricks from the suit. Even if the finesse loses, declarer will have established the three tricks needed. However, West is the dangerous opponent. West has led a heart and, once the ♥A is driven out, the defenders may have enough heart tricks to defeat the contract on gaining the lead.

Declarer holds up winning the ♥A until the third round. Now East has no more hearts and is the safe opponent. Declarer then crosses to the South hand with a spade and takes the club finesse. Even if the finesse loses, which it does, it is to East. If West started with five or more hearts, East will have no heart to lead. If West started with only four hearts, East will have a heart, but the contract is safe since the defenders get only three heart tricks.

If East returns a diamond after winning the ♣K, declarer wins the ♦A and takes the winners.

CONCLUSION

Watch out for the opponents. If one opponent is dangerous and a trick must be lost, try to make sure it is lost to the safe opponent and not the dangerous opponent.

DEAL #6

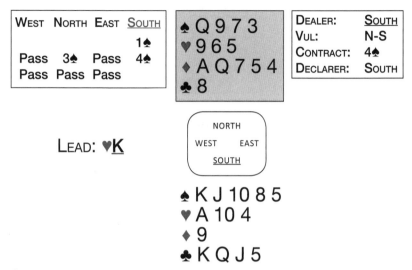

WEST	NORTH	EAST	SOUTH
			1♠
Pass	3♠	Pass	4♠
Pass	Pass	Pass	

♠ Q 9 7 3
♥ 9 6 5
♦ A Q 7 5 4
♣ 8

DEALER:	SOUTH
VUL:	N-S
CONTRACT:	4♠
DECLARER:	SOUTH

LEAD: ♥**K**

NORTH
WEST   EAST
SOUTH

♠ K J 10 8 5
♥ A 10 4
♦ 9
♣ K Q J 5

SUGGESTED BIDDING

South opens 1♠. North, with four-card spade support, revalues the hand as 8 high-card points plus 3 dummy points for the singleton club, a total of 11 points. That's enough to make an invitational *limit raise* to 3♠. South, with 15 points, accepts the invitation and bids 4♠.

OPENING LEAD

West leads the ♥K against 4♠.

PLANNING THE PLAY

Declarer has a sure spade loser, two potential heart losers, and a sure club loser. That's one too many.

BRIDGE QUIZ:

How does declarer plan to eliminate one loser?

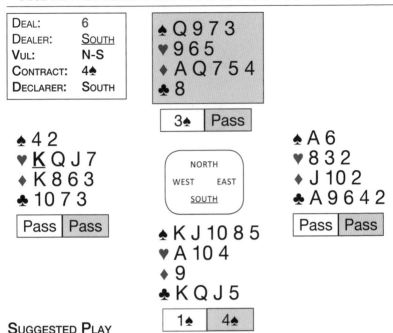

DEAL:	6
DEALER:	SOUTH
VUL:	N-S
CONTRACT:	4♠
DECLARER:	SOUTH

♠ Q 9 7 3
♥ 9 6 5
♦ A Q 7 5 4
♣ 8

| 3♠ | Pass |

♠ 4 2
♥ K Q J 7
♦ K 8 6 3
♣ 10 7 3

NORTH
WEST   EAST
SOUTH

♠ A 6
♥ 8 3 2
♦ J 10 2
♣ A 9 6 4 2

| Pass | Pass |

| Pass | Pass |

♠ K J 10 8 5
♥ A 10 4
♦ 9
♣ K Q J 5

| 1♠ | 4♠ |

SUGGESTED PLAY

After the ♥K lead, declarer cannot lead a spade or a club, and give up the lead to the defenders, before eliminating a heart loser. The only chance is to win the ♥A and immediately take the diamond finesse. When the finesse works, declarer discards a heart loser on the ♦A. Then declarer can start drawing trumps.

If the finesse had lost, declarer would have created a fifth loser and would go down two. The objective is to make the contract. Also, declarer can't afford to promote club winners by giving up the lead because there are too many quick losers.

CONCLUSION

The heart lead is best for the defense since it immediately establishes two potential heart winners. If declarer doesn't eliminate a heart loser before leading a spade or a club, the defense can take four tricks.

If West leads a diamond or a club, declarer would not need to risk the diamond finesse. Two of dummy's hearts could be discarded on South's club winners, after driving out the ♣A.

DEAL #7

WEST	NORTH	EAST	SOUTH
			1♥
Pass	3♥	Pass	4♥
Pass	Pass	Pass	

♠ A 7 4
♥ K 10 8 7
♦ 8 7 6
♣ A 7 2

DEALER:	SOUTH
VUL:	N-S
CONTRACT:	4♥
DECLARER:	SOUTH

LEAD: ♠J

NORTH
WEST   EAST
SOUTH

♠ 6 5 2
♥ A Q 9 6 5 4
♦ A Q
♣ Q 5

SUGGESTED BIDDING

South has 14 high-card points plus 2 length points for the six-card heart suit and opens 1♥. North, with 11 high-card points and four-card heart support, makes an invitational limit raise to 3♥. South has enough strength to continue to game.

OPENING LEAD

West leads the ♠J against 4♥.

PLANNING THE PLAY

Declarer has two spade losers, a diamond loser, and a club loser. One loser must be eliminated.

BRIDGE QUIZ:

How does declarer create a 75% chance of making 4♥?

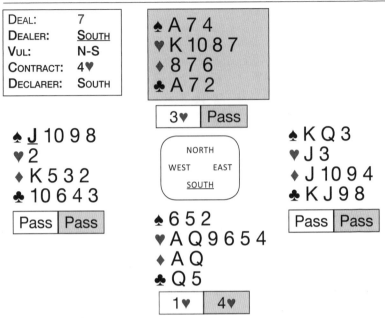

DEAL:	7
DEALER:	SOUTH
VUL:	N-S
CONTRACT:	4♥
DECLARER:	SOUTH

♠ A 7 4
♥ K 10 8 7
♦ 8 7 6
♣ A 7 2

| 3♥ | Pass |

NORTH

WEST EAST

SOUTH

♠ J 10 9 8
♥ 2
♦ K 5 3 2
♣ 10 6 4 3

| Pass | Pass |

♠ K Q 3
♥ J 3
♦ J 10 9 4
♣ K J 9 8

| Pass | Pass |

♠ 6 5 2
♥ A Q 9 6 5 4
♦ A Q
♣ Q 5

| 1♥ | 4♥ |

SUGGESTED PLAY

To have a 75% chance of making the contract, declarer has to try both the diamond and the club finesses. Declarer starts with the club finesse, taking the losses early.

Declarer wins the ♠A and draws trumps in two rounds, ending in dummy. Declarer then leads a low club toward the ♣Q. On the actual deal, if East plays low, declarer won't have a club loser. If East wins the ♣K, East can take two spade winners and shift to the ♦J. Declarer wins the ♦A, takes a trick with the ♣Q, and crosses to dummy with a heart to play the ♣A and discard the ♦Q.

If West held the ♣K and the finesse loses, declarer can still fall back on the diamond finesse. If declarer starts with the diamond finesse, however, and it loses, declarer can no longer fall back on the club finesse, because West will play the ♣K to defeat the contract.

CONCLUSION

If possible, declarer tries to combine chances. Here, declarer has a 75% chance of success by starting with the club finesse – taking the losses early. That leaves the diamond finesse in reserve.

Deal #8

West	North	East	South
			1NT
Pass	Pass	Pass	

♠ A Q J 4
♥ 7 4
♦ 9 6 4
♣ 7 5 4 2

Dealer:	South
Vul:	E-W
Contract:	1NT
Declarer:	South

Lead: ♠**7**

NORTH
WEST   EAST
SOUTH

♠ 6 2
♥ Q J 5 3
♦ A K 7 3
♣ A Q 6

Suggested Bidding

South opens 1NT with a balanced hand and 16 high-card points. North, with only 7 high-card points, passes and stops in partscore.

Opening Lead

West leads the ♠7 against 1NT.

Planning the Play

Declarer has one sure spade trick, two diamonds, and a club. Three more tricks are needed.

Bridge Quiz:

Assume the spade finesse is working. What is the best chance for declarer to get seven tricks?

DEAL:	8
DEALER:	SOUTH
VUL:	E-W
CONTRACT:	1NT
DECLARER:	SOUTH

♠ A Q J 4
♥ 7 4
♦ 9 6 4
♣ 7 5 4 2

Pass

NORTH

WEST   EAST

SOUTH

♠ K 10 8 7 5
♥ K 9 2
♦ 2
♣ K 10 9 3

Pass

♠ 9 3
♥ A 10 8 6
♦ Q J 10 8 5
♣ J 8

Pass

♠ 6 2
♥ Q J 5 3
♦ A K 7 3
♣ A Q 6

1NT

SUGGESTED PLAY

West holds the ♠K, so declarer can get two extra spade tricks. One more could come from a successful club finesse, a 50% chance.

The best odds for the seventh trick, however, comes from taking a repeated heart finesse. Leading twice toward the ♥Q-J gives declarer a 75% chance of an extra trick.

After winning the ♠J at trick one, declarer leads a low heart from dummy. Assuming East plays low, declarer plays the ♥Q or ♥J, losing to West's ♥K. When West leads another spade, declarer wins dummy's ♠Q. With no more entries to dummy, declarer takes the ♠A before leading another heart. Whether or not East plays the ♥A, declarer gets a seventh trick with the ♥Q sooner or later.

CONCLUSION

When declarer can't combine chances, declarer should go with the one that offers the best odds. The repeated heart finesse works if East has the ♥A, the ♥K, or both the ♥A and ♥K. A 75% chance of success. It doesn't work only if West holds both the ♥A and ♥K.

Deal #9

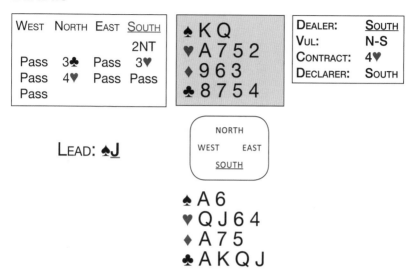

West	North	East	South
			2NT
Pass	3♣	Pass	3♥
Pass	4♥	Pass	Pass
Pass			

♠ K Q
♥ A 7 5 2
♦ 9 6 3
♣ 8 7 5 4

Dealer:	South
Vul:	N-S
Contract:	4♥
Declarer:	South

Lead: ♠J

NORTH
WEST   EAST
SOUTH

♠ A 6
♥ Q J 6 4
♦ A 7 5
♣ A K Q J

Suggested Bidding

South, with 21 high-card points and a balanced hand, opens 2NT. North checks for a major-suit fit by using the Stayman convention. When South shows a four-card or longer heart suit, North raises to 4♥.

Opening Lead

West leads the ♠J against 4♥.

Planning the Play

There are two diamond losers, so declarer can afford one heart loser.

Bridge Quiz:

In which hand should declarer win the first spade trick?

How does declarer plan to play hearts?

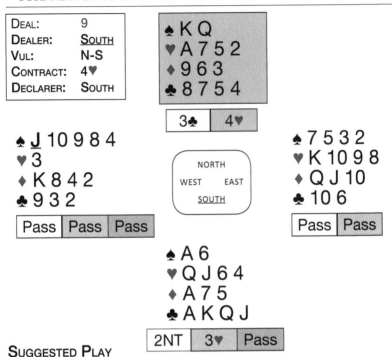

DEAL:	9
DEALER:	SOUTH
VUL:	N-S
CONTRACT:	4♥
DECLARER:	SOUTH

♠ K Q
♥ A 7 5 2
♦ 9 6 3
♣ 8 7 5 4

3♣   4♥

♠ J 10 9 8 4
♥ 3
♦ K 8 4 2
♣ 9 3 2

NORTH
WEST   EAST
SOUTH

♠ 7 5 3 2
♥ K 10 9 8
♦ Q J 10
♣ 10 6

Pass	Pass	Pass

Pass	Pass

♠ A 6
♥ Q J 6 4
♦ A 7 5
♣ A K Q J

2NT   3♥   Pass

SUGGESTED PLAY

Declarer wins the first trick with the ♠A, keeping the ♠6 as a *link card* to get to the dummy. If hearts are divided 3-2, declarer loses only one trick to the ♥K. The hearts could be divided 4-1, however, if West started with four hearts including the ♥K, there's nothing declarer can do to avoid two heart losers. In this deal, it's East who has four cards. The focus is on how to play the heart suit to guard against a 4-1 break, with East holding four hearts to the ♥K.

Declarer should start with dummy's ♥A in case either defender holds a singleton ♥K. When both defenders follow with low hearts, declarer leads low toward the ♥Q-J. On the actual deal, East can play low and let South win the ♥J. Declarer then crosses back to the ♠K in dummy to lead another heart toward the ♥Q. East gets only one trick, the ♥K.

CONCLUSION

Declarer should lead an honor if declarer can afford to have it covered by a defender's higher honor. Otherwise, declarer should usually lead toward the honor.

DEAL #10

WEST	NORTH	EAST	SOUTH
	1♦	1♠	1NT
Pass	2NT	Pass	3NT
Pass	Pass	Pass	

♠ 6 5
♥ A Q 10 7
♦ A K Q J
♣ Q 8 2

DEALER:	NORTH
VUL:	BOTH
CONTRACT:	3NT
DECLARER:	SOUTH

LEAD: ♠2

♠ K 10 9
♥ J 9 2
♦ 10 6
♣ K J 10 7 3

SUGGESTED BIDDING

North's balanced hand with 18 high-card points is too strong to open 1NT. North starts with 1♦. East overcalls 1♠. South has 8 high-card points plus 1 length point for the five-card club suit. With a spade *stopper*, South responds 1NT. North raises to 2NT, showing a balanced hand and about 18-19 points. With the top of the range for the 1NT response, South accepts the invitation.

OPENING LEAD

West leads the ♠2 against 3NT.

PLANNING THE PLAY

Declarer will get a trick with the ♠K and has a heart and four diamonds. Three more tricks are needed.

BRIDGE QUIZ:

How can declarer get the extra tricks needed to make the contract?

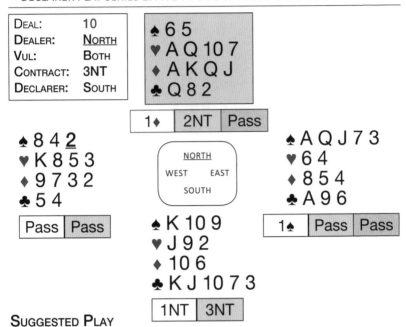

DEAL:	10
DEALER:	NORTH
VUL:	BOTH
CONTRACT:	3NT
DECLARER:	SOUTH

♠ 6 5
♥ A Q 10 7
♦ A K Q J
♣ Q 8 2

| 1♦ | 2NT | Pass |

♠ 8 4 <u>2</u>
♥ K 8 5 3
♦ 9 7 3 2
♣ 5 4

NORTH
WEST   EAST
SOUTH

♠ A Q J 7 3
♥ 6 4
♦ 8 5 4
♣ A 9 6

| Pass | Pass |

♠ K 10 9
♥ J 9 2
♦ 10 6
♣ K J 10 7 3

| 1♠ | Pass | Pass |

| 1NT | 3NT |

SUGGESTED PLAY

One possibility is to promote clubs, but that lets East gain the lead with the ♣A and take the defenders' established spade winners to defeat the contract. Instead, declarer will need to get the extra tricks from hearts, hoping West holds the ♥K.

The heart card combination must be handled carefully. After winning the ♠K, declarer should lead the ♥9, not the ♥J because there are entry problems. If West plays low, declarer plays dummy's ♥7. Declarer continues with the ♥J. If West plays low again, declarer is still on lead after the ♥J wins and can take a third finesse.

If declarer were to start with the ♥J, West should play low – there's nothing to gain by covering. The ♥J wins. Declarer can take another finesse, but this trick is won by dummy's ♥Q or ♥10. Now declarer is in the wrong hand to repeat the finesse a third time.

CONCLUSION

By considering that both defenders are dangerous, after declarer plays the ♠K, and the defenders have enough quick tricks to defeat the contract, declarer can determine the opponents can't be given the lead. Therefore, declarer chooses the heart finesse for the extra tricks.

DEAL #11

WEST	NORTH	EAST	SOUTH
			2NT
Pass	3NT	Pass	Pass
Pass			

♠ 9 5 3
♥ K 6 3
♦ 6 4 3
♣ K 5 3 2

DEALER:	SOUTH
VUL:	N-S
CONTRACT:	3NT
DECLARER:	SOUTH

LEAD: ♥**5**

```
          NORTH
    WEST        EAST
          SOUTH
```

♠ K 7 6
♥ A 8
♦ A Q 10
♣ A Q J 10 6

SUGGESTED BIDDING

South opens 2NT, with a balanced hand and 20 high-card points plus 1 length point for the five-card club suit. North, with a balanced hand and 6 high-card points, raises to 3NT.

OPENING LEAD

West leads the ♥5 against 3NT.

PLANNING THE PLAY

Declarer starts with two hearts, a diamond, and five clubs. That's eight tricks. One more is needed.

BRIDGE QUIZ:

What are the odds of declarer getting one more trick?

DEAL:	11
DEALER:	SOUTH
VUL:	N-S
CONTRACT:	3NT
DECLARER:	SOUTH

♠ 9 5 3
♥ K 6 3
♦ 6 4 3
♣ K 5 3 2

3NT

NORTH

WEST   EAST

SOUTH

♠ A 4 2
♥ Q 10 7 5 2
♦ K 9 5
♣ 9 4

Pass   Pass

♠ Q J 10 8
♥ J 9 4
♦ J 8 7 2
♣ 8 7

Pass

♠ K 7 6
♥ A 8
♦ A Q 10
♣ A Q J 10 6

2NT   Pass

SUGGESTED PLAY

One possibility is the spade finesse, hoping East holds the ♠A. That's a 50% chance. Another possibility is the diamond finesse. By starting with a low diamond to the ♦10, planning to follow with a low diamond to the ♦Q if the first finesse loses to the ♦J, declarer has a 75% chance of getting an extra trick. It provides at least one extra trick if East holds the ♦K, or the ♦J, or both the ♦K and ♦J. It only loses if West holds both the ♦K and ♦J.

On this deal, the first finesse of the ♦10 drives out the ♦K, giving declarer nine tricks on regaining the lead.

If declarer starts by playing a diamond and finessing the ♦Q, losing to West's ♦K, declarer can later finesse the ♦10 to make the contract. Playing this way, however, declarer gives up the chance for an overtrick if East holds both the ♦K and ♦J.

CONCLUSION

When chances can't be combined, declarer chooses the suit that offers the best odds. A card combination that requires only one of two cards to be favorably placed offers better odds than a suit that requires one card to be favorably placed.

DEAL #12

WEST	NORTH	EAST	SOUTH
			1NT
Pass	3NT	Pass	Pass
Pass			

♠ A 7 5
♥ 8 6 3
♦ A Q 4 2
♣ K 7 4

DEALER:	SOUTH
VUL:	NONE
CONTRACT:	3NT
DECLARER:	SOUTH

LEAD: ♠J

♠ K Q 4
♥ A K 4 2
♦ 10 3
♣ A 6 3 2

SUGGESTED BIDDING

South opens 1NT with 16 high-card points and a balanced hand. North has 13 high-card points, enough to raise right to 3NT.

OPENING LEAD

West leads the ♠J against 3NT.

PLANNING THE PLAY

Declarer has three spades, two hearts, a diamond, and two clubs. One more trick is needed to make the contract.

BRIDGE QUIZ:

How can declarer create a better than 50% chance of making the contract?

DEAL:	12
DEALER:	SOUTH
VUL:	NONE
CONTRACT:	3NT
DECLARER:	SOUTH

♠ A 7 5
♥ 8 6 3
♦ A Q 4 2
♣ K 7 4

3NT

NORTH
WEST   EAST
SOUTH

♠ J 10 9 8   ♠ 6 3 2
♥ J 10 7 5   ♥ Q 9
♦ 8 6 5   ♦ K J 9 7
♣ Q 8   ♣ J 10 9 5

Pass Pass   Pass

♠ K Q 4
♥ A K 4 2
♦ 10 3
♣ A 6 3 2

1NT Pass

SUGGESTED PLAY

Declarer can try to establish an extra heart trick through length by giving up a heart and hoping the missing hearts divide 3-3. The odds of that are about 36%. Declarer has the same possibility in clubs. Another 36% chance. The straightforward diamond finesse is a 50% chance. However, declarer can take two finesses in diamonds, giving declarer a 75% chance of making the contract.

Declarer wins the first trick in dummy with the ♠A, and leads a low diamond toward the ♦10. On the actual deal, East will likely win the ♦J. On regaining the lead, declarer plays the ♦10, losing a trick to East's ♦K. Dummy's ♦Q has been established as the ninth trick.

If East were to play a low diamond on the first round and South's ♦10 lost to the ♦J in West's hand, declarer still has the second chance of finessing the ♦Q. Declarer's play wins if West holds the ♦K and ♦J, if West holds the ♦K and East the ♦J, or if East holds the ♦K and ♦J. It loses only if West holds the ♦J and East the ♦K.

CONCLUSION

10s and 9s – and even lower-ranking cards – can play an important role in handling particular card combinations.

DEAL #13

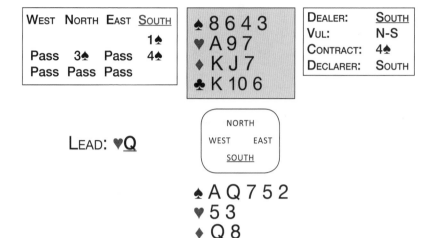

WEST	NORTH	EAST	SOUTH
			1♠
Pass	3♠	Pass	4♠
Pass	Pass	Pass	

♠ 8 6 4 3
♥ A 9 7
♦ K J 7
♣ K 10 6

DEALER:	SOUTH
VUL:	N-S
CONTRACT:	4♠
DECLARER:	SOUTH

LEAD: ♥Q

NORTH
WEST   EAST
SOUTH

♠ A Q 7 5 2
♥ 5 3
♦ Q 8
♣ A Q J 8

SUGGESTED BIDDING

South opens 1♠ with a semi-balanced hand, and 15 high-card points plus 1 length point for the five-card spade suit. North, with four-card spade support and 11 high-card points, bids 3♠, an invitational raise. With more than a minimum opening, South continues to game.

OPENING LEAD

West leads the ♥Q against 4♠.

PLANNING THE PLAY

Declarer has a sure heart loser and a sure diamond loser. Declarer can afford one spade loser but not two.

BRIDGE QUIZ:

How should declarer play spades for only one loser?

DEAL:	13
DEALER:	SOUTH
VUL:	N-S
CONTRACT:	4♠
DECLARER:	SOUTH

North
♠ 8 6 4 3
♥ A 9 7
♦ K J 7
♣ K 10 6

3♠	Pass

NORTH

WEST   EAST

SOUTH

West
♠ K
♥ Q J 10 6
♦ 9 6 5 3
♣ 7 5 4 2

Pass	Pass

East
♠ J 10 9
♥ K 8 4 2
♦ A 10 4 2
♣ 9 3

Pass	Pass

South
♠ A Q 7 5 2
♥ 5 3
♦ Q 8
♣ A Q J 8

1♠	4♠

SUGGESTED PLAY

To play as safely as possible, declarer should play the ♠A on the first round of trumps to guard against West holding the singleton ♠K. On the actual deal, West's singleton ♠K falls. Declarer takes a second spade trick with the ♠Q, and eventually loses only one spade trick to East.

If West had followed with a low spade rather than the ♠K when declarer leads the ♠A, declarer would cross to dummy and lead toward the ♠Q. Declarer makes the contract whenever spades are divided 2-2, whenever West has a singleton ♠K, and whenever spades are divided 3-1 with East holding three spades. 4♠ goes down only if West started with three spades including the ♠K, or spades divide 4-0. In those cases, there's nothing declarer can do.

CONCLUSION

When deciding the best way to handle a card combination, declarer should consider whether it is better to start by leading a high card or by leading toward a high card. How declarer handles a particular card combination can depend on how many tricks are needed from the suit.

DEAL #14

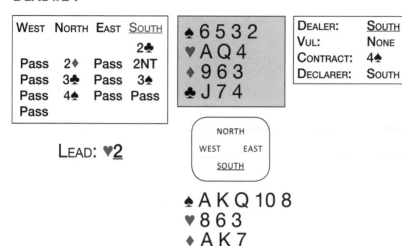

WEST	NORTH	EAST	SOUTH
			2♣
Pass	2♦	Pass	2NT
Pass	3♣	Pass	3♠
Pass	4♠	Pass	Pass
Pass			

♠ 6 5 3 2
♥ A Q 4
♦ 9 6 3
♣ J 7 4

DEALER:	SOUTH
VUL:	NONE
CONTRACT:	4♠
DECLARER:	SOUTH

LEAD: ♥2

NORTH
WEST   EAST
SOUTH

♠ A K Q 10 8
♥ 8 6 3
♦ A K 7
♣ A Q

SUGGESTED BIDDING

South opens 2♣ with 22 high-card points plus 1 length point for the five-card spade suit. North makes a 2♦ *waiting bid*. South rebids 2NT, showing a balanced hand with about 22-24 points. North decides to use Stayman. South shows a four-card or longer spade suit. North raises to 4♠.

OPENING LEAD

West leads the ♥2 against 4♠.

PLANNING THE PLAY

Assuming West doesn't have all four missing spades, declarer has no spade losers but two potential heart losers, one diamond, and one club loser.

BRIDGE QUIZ:

Should declarer play hearts or clubs to get an extra trick?

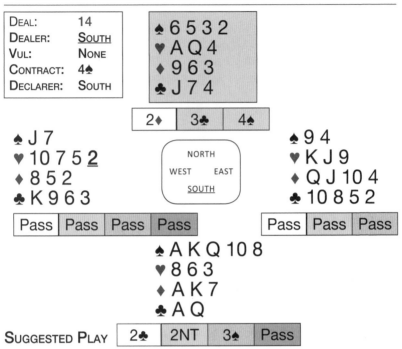

Deal:	14
Dealer:	South
Vul:	None
Contract:	4♠
Declarer:	South

♠ 6 5 3 2
♥ A Q 4
♦ 9 6 3
♣ J 7 4

2♦	3♣	4♠

♠ J 7
♥ 10 7 5 2
♦ 8 5 2
♣ K 9 6 3

NORTH
WEST   EAST
SOUTH

♠ 9 4
♥ K J 9
♦ Q J 10 4
♣ 10 8 5 2

Pass	Pass	Pass	Pass

Pass	Pass	Pass

♠ A K Q 10 8
♥ 8 6 3
♦ A K 7
♣ A Q

Suggested Play	2♣	2NT	3♠	Pass

Declarer could avoid a heart loser by playing dummy's ♥Q, hoping West holds the ♥K. Similarly, a club loser might be avoided with a successful club finesse. If the club finesse loses, dummy's ♣J will become a winner on which the diamond loser can be discarded.

However, declarer has only one sure entry to dummy, the ♥A. If declarer tries the heart finesse and it loses, the defenders can drive out the ♥A and declarer will be left with no entry to dummy.

At trick one, declarer should play a low heart from dummy. East wins the ♥J but can't lead another heart without giving declarer two heart tricks. East will switch to the ♦Q, top of the sequence. Declarer wins and draws trumps. Declarer now plays the ♣A and continues with the ♣Q, giving up a trick to the ♣K. That establishes dummy's ♣J as a winner and the ♥A is still there as an entry. Declarer no longer needs the heart finesse. A heart can be discarded on the ♣J.

Conclusion

The plan is to promote the ♣J as a winner in the dummy.

DEAL #15 – FAMOUS DEAL

WEST	NORTH	EAST	SOUTH
	1♥	Pass	2♠
Pass	3♠	Pass	4NT
Pass	5♦	Pass	6♠
Pass	Pass	Pass	

♠ K 9 8
♥ A K J 5 3
♦ Q J 7
♣ 8 3

DEALER:	NORTH
VUL:	N-S
CONTRACT:	6♠
DECLARER:	SOUTH

LEAD: ♦10

NORTH
WEST   EAST
SOUTH

♠ A Q J 10 7 3
♥ 7 6
♦ K 5 4
♣ A Q

SUGGESTED BIDDING

Many North players would open 1NT with a balanced hand and 14 high-card points plus 1 length point for the five-card heart suit. However, the range for 1NT was 16-18 points when this famous deal was played. So North opened 1♥. South responded 2♠, a strong jump shift, with 16 high-card points plus 2 length points for the six-card spade suit. North raised spades bidding 3♠. South used the Blackwood convention and upon discovering the partnership was missing an ace, settled for a small slam, bidding 6♠.

OPENING LEAD

West leads the ♦10 against 6♠.

PLANNING THE PLAY

Declarer can afford one loser and has a sure diamond loser and a potential club loser.

BRIDGE QUIZ:

How does declarer try to avoid a club loser?

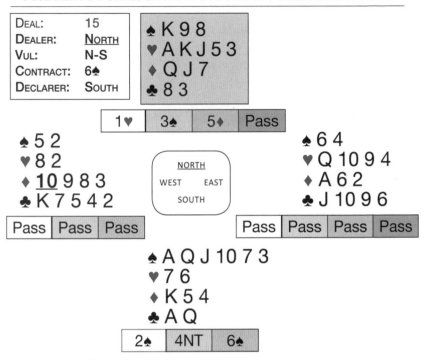

Deal:	15
Dealer:	North
Vul:	N-S
Contract:	6♠
Declarer:	South

♠ K 9 8
♥ A K J 5 3
♦ Q J 7
♣ 8 3

1♥	3♠	5♦	Pass

♠ 5 2
♥ 8 2
♦ **10** 9 8 3
♣ K 7 5 4 2

NORTH
WEST EAST
SOUTH

♠ 6 4
♥ Q 10 9 4
♦ A 6 2
♣ J 10 9 6

Pass	Pass	Pass

Pass	Pass	Pass	Pass

♠ A Q J 10 7 3
♥ 7 6
♦ K 5 4
♣ A Q

2♠	4NT	6♠

Suggested Play

To avoid the club loser, one possibility is the 50% club finesse. There's a better option. Declarer can try to establish an extra heart winner on which to discard the ♣Q. When East wins the ♦A, South unblocks the ♦K to leave the ♦Q and ♦J as entries to dummy. When East shifts to the ♣J, declarer wins the ♣A and draws two rounds of trumps. Then, declarer plays the ♥A, ♥K, and ruffs a third heart. The ♥Q doesn't fall so declarer crosses to dummy with a spade or diamond, and ruffs another heart, bringing down the ♥Q. Declarer crosses back to dummy again and plays the ♥J, discarding the ♣Q.

Conclusion

The odds of the six missing hearts dividing either 3-3 or 4-2 are about 85% - much better than the 50% odds of the club finesse working.

This deal was played by Dwight D. Eisenhower and is the first deal to ever appear on the front page of Time Magazine which did an extensive article on the president's fondness for the game.

DEAL #16 – FAMOUS DEAL

West	North	East	South
	1♣	Pass	1♠
Pass	1NT	Pass	4♠
Pass	Pass	Pass	

♠ 7 4
♥ Q 10 9 6
♦ A K 2
♣ K Q 5 4

Dealer:	North
Vul:	E-W
Contract:	4♠
Declarer:	South

LEAD: ♦J

♠ A Q 6 5 3 2
♥ K 5
♦ 8 5
♣ A 6 2

SUGGESTED BIDDING

North opens 1♣, the longer minor, with a balanced hand and 14 high-card points. South has enough to take the partnership to game after North opens but starts by bidding the spade suit at the one level. With only two spades, North rebids 1NT, to show a minimum balanced hand. South now knows the partnership has at least an eight-card spade fit and puts the partnership in 4♠.

OPENING LEAD

West leads the ♦J against 4♠.

PLANNING THE PLAY

Declarer can afford three losers and has one heart loser, no diamond losers, and no club loser. Declarer can afford two spade losers but not three.

BRIDGE QUIZ:

How does declarer plan to play spades, the trump suit, for only two losers?

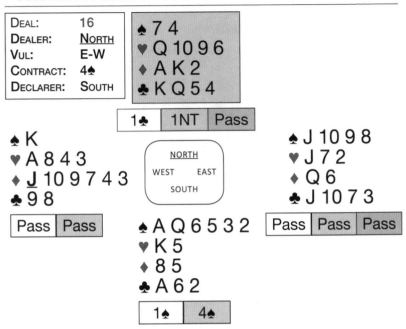

Suggested Play

If declarer finesses the ♠Q, declarer will have three spade losers, the ♠K, ♠J, and ♠10. Declarer can afford to start playing spades by starting with the ♠A. Then, declarer loses only two spade tricks, the ♠J and ♠10, this is called a safety play. As long as East doesn't show out, declarer can't lose more than two spades.

Only if West started with four spades, including the ♠K, would declarer have three spade losers. If that were the case, there would be nothing declarer could do, even if declarer tried the spade finesse.

Conclusion

The safety play doesn't cost anything and may be the only way declarer can make the contract. When handling a card combination, consider whether you can afford to start by playing a high card.

This deal was played by Winston Churchill, a bridge enthusiast, who started playing before the days of contract bridge.

Opening Lead Guidelines

LEADS AGAINST NOTRUMP

If partner has bid a suit:

- Lead the top of a doubleton (♠7-2, ♦J-5)
- Lead the top of touching honors (♥Q-J-6)
- With no sequence, lead low (♣J-7-6-3 ♥K-8-5)
- If you raised, you can lead the top of nothing (♦8-6-3)

Otherwise, lead the longest suit:

- Lead top of touching honors from a sequence:
  o A solid sequence (♥K-Q-J-7-4)
  o A broken sequence (♠J-10-8-6-3)
  o An interior sequence (♦A-J-10-7-2)
- With no sequence, lead fourth highest

With a choice of suits:

- Lead the stronger
- Lead the unbid suit

If leading a long suit is unattractive because you have no entry or it was bid by the opponents, an alternative is leading top of nothing.

LEADS AGAINST A SUIT

Choosing the suit:

- Partner's suit
- An unbid suit
- A singleton or doubleton (if partner is likely to gain the lead before trumps are drawn)
- A long suit, hoping to force declarer to trump
- A trump, if declarer is likely to trump losers in dummy or all other leads are unattractive

Choosing the suit:

- Lead the top of a doubleton (♠8-2, ♥Q-4)
- Lead the top of touching honors (♦K-Q-5)
- Lead the ace (♣A-J-8-5-3)
- Lead low from an honor (♥K-J-7-4, ♠Q-9-2)

Glossary

Card Combination—A combined holding in a suit between the partnership hands. (Page 1)

Dangerous Opponent—An opponent declarer does not want to see gain the lead. The opponent may have winners to take or be able to make a damaging lead that could defeat the contract. (Page 15)

Declarer's Plan—When the opening lead is made, and dummy appears, declarer should make a plan for taking enough tricks to make the contract. There are three stages: Assess the Situation, Browse Declarer's Checklist, and Consider the Order. (Page 2)

Discard(ing)—Play a card to a trick that is from a different suit than the one led and is not a trump. (Page 2)

Entry—A way to get from one hand to the opposite hand. (Page 1)

Finesse—A method of building extra tricks by trapping an opponent's high card(s). (Page 1)

Hold Up—Letting the opponents win a trick that you could win. (Page 16)

Honor—An ace, king, queen, jack or ten. (Page 11)

Length—The number of cards held in a suit. Also, the development of tricks through exhausting the cards the opponents hold in a suit. (Page 2)

Limit Raise—A raise of partner's suit from the one level to the three level that invites partner to continue to game. (Page 31)

Link Card—A card that can be led to a winner (entry) in the opposite hand. (Page 38)

Loser—A trick which might be lost to the opponents. (Page 2)

Promotion—Developing one or more cards into winners by driving out any higher-ranking cards held by the opponents. (Page 2)

Quick Loser—A trick that the opponents are ready to take upon gaining the lead. (Page 18)

Ruff(ing) (Trumping)—Play a trump to a trick when holding no cards in the suit led. (Page 2)

Safe Opponent—An opponent to whom declarer does not mind losing a trick. The opponent is not able to immediately make a damaging lead that could defeat the contract. (Page 15)

Slow Loser—A trick that may eventually have to be lost but that the opponents can't immediately take upon gaining the lead. (Page 18)

Stayman (Convention)—An artificial 2♣ response to an opening 1NT bid, or 3♣ to an opening 2NT bid, asking if opener has a four-card major suit. (Page 23)

Stopper—A holding that is likely to prevent the opponents from immediately taking all the tricks in the suit. (Page 39)

Suit Preference Signal—A defensive signal made when leading or following suit that indicates preference for another suit. (Page 3)

Sure Trick—A trick that can be taken without giving up the lead to the opponents. (Page 1)

Two Diamond (2♦) Waiting Bid—An artificial response of 2♦ to an opening 2♣ bid saying nothing about responder's hand. Responder is leaving room for opener to describe the hand. (Page 47)

Winner—A card held by one of the players that will win a trick when it is played. (Page 2)

Notes

Notes

Notes